Make a Difference

written by J.C. Bates

illustrated by Felipe Galindo

**McGraw-Hill
School Division**

New York   Farmington

The environment is a lot like the weather. People spend time talking about it. Some people shake their heads and say that nothing can be done about it, so why bother?

Unlike the weather, people have control over how they care for the environment. People can limit the amount of water and electricity they use. This is called conserving, or saving, energy.

Conserving Water

To keep your teeth healthy, you should brush them after you eat. How much water do you waste when you leave the water running while you brush?

You waste 10 gallons of water each day. That's 3,650 gallons every year. If you have four people in your family, that's enough water to fill a swimming pool!

TIP: Wet your toothbrush. Then turn off the faucet while you brush. Rinse it at the end.

A toilet uses five to seven gallons of water every time you flush. Even if you only flushed once a day, you would still be using about 2,500 gallons of water each year.

Drip, drip, drip. Not only is a dripping faucet annoying, but it's also a terrible waste of water. One drop of water adds up to about 200 gallons each day. That's the same as flushing a toilet 40 times.

TIP: Make sure you turn off the faucet completely. Tell somebody if it's dripping. Do this not just at home, but anywhere you notice a leaky faucet.

Everybody loves a bubble bath. But each time you take a bath, you use a lot of water. It takes about 20 gallons of water to fill a bathtub. Even if you only took one bath a week, you'd use over a 1,000 gallons of water each year.

TIP: Take a shower instead of a bath. Showers use less water. Make your showers as short as possible, but be sure you wash behind your ears!

Conserving Electricity

In the United States, more than half the electricity we use is made by burning coal. Coal is a cheap source of energy, but it's bad for Earth. Coal mines have to be dug deeper and deeper, which tears up the land and destroys the soil. When coal burns, it releases poisons into the air. These poisons can cause acid rain, which harms every living thing on Earth.

Electrical appliance	Pounds of coal
Water heater......................3,375	
Oven 560	
TV...25	
Hair dryer................................20	
Vacuum cleaner 37	

Look at the chart above. Notice how much coal it takes for a family of four to run different appliances each year.

TIP: Limit your use of appliances, especially those that use lots of heat. You may want to turn off the TV, and take a bike ride instead.

TIP: Create a Last-Person-Out-of-the-Room policy at your house. Explain that the last person to leave the room is responsible for turning off everything that's not being used. This includes lights, fans, radios, and televisions.

Every year people in the United States use more electricity to run their air conditioners than China uses to run their whole country. And China has about four times as many people as the United States!

TIP: Fans use a tiny amount of energy compared to air conditioners. Fans are also a lot less noisy. Use them instead.

Keeping Cool in the Summer

Think about the Sun and how much heat it produces. To stay cool when it's hot outside, you could go swimming or diving at your community pool. But how can you keep cool inside your house, without turning up the air conditioner?

TIP: Plant trees or bushes in front of
windows and along the sides of your house.
Not only will plants make everything look
prettier, but they will also help block the
Sun's rays.

TIP: Pull down the shades, shut the
blinds, or close the curtains. The less
sunlight you let enter the windows, the
cooler your house will be.

Keeping Warm in the Winter

In the winter you want to have as much heat as possible in order to stay warm. But there are still ways you can conserve energy!

TIP: Open the curtains, blinds, or shades to let in the Sun. It will help warm the house.

It's snowing outside, the wind is blowing, and you're feeling chilly. Don't turn up the heat!

TIP: Put on a nice, warm sweater. Slip on some wooly socks. Have some hot cocoa!

Long ago, when the United States was made up of villages instead of large cities, people used much less energy than they do today. Today our energy use comes in the form of heating, lighting, transportation, and the production of goods.

There are plenty of things one person can do to make a difference. Conservation doesn't take much energy, but it saves a lot of it.